Classic Tales

Level 1

T0364343

The Enormous Turnip

Retold by Sue Arengo
Illustrated by Adrienne Salgado

Contents

OXFORD
UNIVERSITY PRESS

 The man's got a seed. He goes in the garden. He puts the seed in the ground.

The seed grows. The man's happy.

The seed grows and grows.
It's a turnip.

The turnip's big. It's very big.

The man's very happy.

'It's big,' he says.

The man's hungry. He wants to eat the turnip.

The man pulls the turnip. The turnip doesn't move.

The man sees the
woman.

'Come and help!'
he says.

'Pull!' says the man.

The woman pulls the
man. The man pulls
the turnip.

The turnip doesn't
move.

Pull!

They see a boy.

'Come and help!' they say.

'Pull!' says the woman.

The boy pulls the woman. The woman pulls the man. The man pulls the turnip.

The turnip doesn't move.

Pull!

They see a girl.

'Come and help!' they say.

Come and help!

'Pull!' says the boy.

The girl pulls the boy. The boy pulls the woman. The woman pulls the man. The man pulls the turnip.

The turnip doesn't move.

Pull!

They see a dog.

'Come and help!' they say.

'Pull!' says the girl.

The dog pulls the girl. The girl pulls the boy. The boy pulls the woman. The woman pulls the man. The man pulls the turnip.

They pull and they pull. The turnip doesn't move.

They see the cat.

'Come and help!' they say.

'Pull!' says the man.

The cat pulls the dog. The dog pulls the girl. The girl pulls the boy. The boy pulls the woman. The woman pulls the man. The man pulls the turnip.

They pull and they pull and they pull. The turnip doesn't move.

Pull!

They see the mouse.

'Come and help!' they say.

'Pull!' says the woman.

The mouse pulls the cat. The cat pulls the dog. The dog pulls the girl. The girl pulls the boy. The boy pulls the woman. The woman pulls the man. The man pulls the turnip.

They pull and they pull and they pull and …

YES!

'We've got the turnip!' they say.
'We've got the enormous turnip!'

'Come and eat!' says the woman.

They eat the turnip.

'It's good!'

1 What do they say? Write the words.

1

It's __big__ .

2

_____!

3

Come and _____!

4

It's _____!

2 Write the words.

1 The __mouse__ pulls the cat.

2 The cat pulls the _____.

3 The _____ pulls the boy.

4 The _____ pulls the man.

5 The man pulls the _____.

3 Write the words and number the sentences 1–6.

turnip   eat   move   man   mouse   ~~ground~~

☐ They _____ the turnip.

☐ The man, the woman, the boy, the girl, the dog, the cat, and the _____ pull the turnip.

☐ The _____ grows and grows.

☐ The _____ pulls the turnip.

1 The man puts a seed in the _ground_ .

☐ The turnip doesn't _____ .

4 Answer the questions.

1 What's this?
It's a turnip.
Is it small?

_____

Is it big?

_____

2 Who is it?

_____

Is he happy?

_____

3 Who is it?

_____

Picture Dictionary

big *It's big.*

enormous *It's enormous.*

boy

garden

cat

girl

dog

ground

eat

grow

happy *He's happy.*

help

hungry *He's hungry.*

man

mouse

move

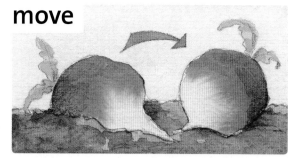

pull

seed

turnip

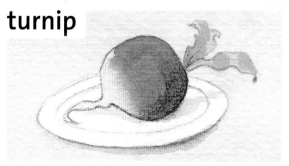

woman

Classic Tales

Classic stories retold for learners of English – bringing the magic of traditional storytelling to the language classroom

For Classic Tales Teacher's Handbook, visit www.oup.com/elt/readers/classictales

Level 1: 100 headwords
- The Enormous Turnip
- The Lazy Grasshopper
- The Little Red Hen
- Lownu Mends the Sky
- The Magic Cooking Pot
- The Magpie and the Milk
- Mansour and the Donkey
- Peach Boy
- The Princess and the Pea
- Rumpelstiltskin
- The Shoemaker and the Elves
- Three Billy-Goats

Level 2: 150 headwords
- Amrita and the Trees
- Big Baby Finn
- The Fisherman and his Wife
- The Gingerbread Man
- Jack and the Beanstalk
- King Arthur and the Sword
- Rainforest Boy
- Thumbelina
- The Town Mouse and the Country Mouse
- The Ugly Duckling

Level 3: 200 headwords
- Aladdin
- Bambi and the Prince of the Forest
- Goldilocks and the Three Bears
- The Heron and the Hummingbird
- The Little Mermaid
- Little Red Riding Hood
- Rapunzel

Level 4: 300 headwords
- Cinderella
- Don Quixote: Adventures of a Spanish Knight
- The Goose Girl
- Sleeping Beauty
- The Twelve Dancing Princesses

Level 5: 400 headwords
- Beauty and the Beast
- The Magic Brocade
- Pinocchio
- Snow White and the Seven Dwarfs

OXFORD
UNIVERSITY PRESS

Great Clarendon Street, Oxford, OX2 6DP, United Kingdom

Oxford University Press is a department of the University of Oxford. It furthers the University's objective of excellence in research, scholarship, and education by publishing worldwide. Oxford is a registered trade mark of Oxford University Press in the UK and in certain other countries

© Oxford University Press 2011

The moral rights of the author have been asserted

First published in 1998

2023

26

ISBN: 978 0 19 423866 3   Book
ISBN: 978 0 19 424000 0   e-Book
ISBN: 978 0 19 423867 0   Activity Book and Play
ISBN: 978 0 19 400274 5   Audio Pack

Printed in China

This book is printed on paper from certified and well-managed sources

ACKNOWLEDGEMENTS

Illustrated by: Adrienne Salgado/The Organisation